All Kinds of
Beliefs

Written by Anita Ganeri

Illustrated by Ayesha Rubio
and Jenny Palmer

CRABTREE
PUBLISHING COMPANY
WWW.CRABTREEBOOKS.COM

CRABTREE
PUBLISHING COMPANY
WWW.CRABTREEBOOKS.COM

Author: Anita Ganeri

Editorial director: Kathy Middleton

Editors: Nicola Edwards, Ellen Rodger

Illustrators: Ayesha Rubio, Jenny Palmer

Proofreader: Crystal Sikkens

Designer: Little Red Ant

Prepress technician: Margaret Salter

Print coordinator: Katherine Berti

Library and Archives Canada Cataloguing in Publication

Title: All kinds of beliefs / written by Anita Ganeri ; illustrated by
 Ayesha Rubio and Jenny Palmer.
Names: Ganeri, Anita, 1961- author. | Rubio, Ayesha L., illustrator. |
 Palmer, Jenny (Illustrator), illustrator.
Description: Series statement: All kinds of people |
 Previously published: London: Franklin Watts, 2019. |
 Includes index.
Identifiers: Canadiana (print) 20190200480 |
 Canadiana (ebook) 20190200499 |
 ISBN 9780778768005 (hardcover) |
 ISBN 9780778768043 (softcover) |
 ISBN 9781427124210 (HTML)
Subjects: LCSH: Faith—Juvenile literature. | LCSH: Religious life—
 Juvenile literature. | LCSH: Religions—Juvenile literature.
Classification: LCC BL92 .G36 2020 | DDC j200—dc23

Library of Congress Cataloging-in-Publication Data

Names: Ganeri, Anita, 1961- author. | Lopez Rubio,
 Ayesha, illustrator. | Palmer, Jenny, illustrator.
Title: All kinds of beliefs / written by Anita Ganeri ; illustrated by
 Ayesha Rubio and Jenny Palmer.
Description: New York, NY : Crabtree Publishing Company, 2020. |
 Series: All kinds of people | Includes index.
Identifiers: LCCN 2019043884 (print) | LCCN 2019043885 (ebook) |
 ISBN 9780778768005 (hardcover) |
 ISBN 9780778768043 (paperback) |
 ISBN 9781427124210 (ebook)
Subjects: LCSH: Religions--Juvenile literature.
Classification: LCC BL92 .G35 2020 (print) | LCC BL92 (ebook) |
 DDC 200--dc23
LC record available at https://lccn.loc.gov/2019043884
LC ebook record available at https://lccn.loc.gov/2019043885

Crabtree Publishing Company
www.crabtreebooks.com   1-800-387-7650
Published by Crabtree Publishing Company in 2020

Published in Canada
Crabtree Publishing
616 Welland Avenue
St. Catharines, ON
L2M 5V6

Published in the United States
Crabtree Publishing
PMB 59051
350 Fifth Ave, 59th Floor
New York, NY 10118

Printed in the U.S.A./012020/CG20191115

First published in Great Britain in 2019 by The Watts Publishing Group
Copyright © The Watts Publishing Group 2019

Contents

Children may learn their beliefs from their parents, or from teachers at their school or place of worship.

People's beliefs guide how they live and behave toward others.

Be kind to other people.

Respect **your** elders.

Treat everyone **as** equal.

Many people believe there is a God
who made everything in the world.

They try to live their lives
as God wants them to.

In Islam, we
call God Allah.

Christians believe
that God sent his son, Jesus,
to Earth to save people.

A religion may have many gods or no god.

Hindus believe in a great spirit, called Brahman. There are also many gods and goddesses.

Buddhists don't have a god. We follow the teachings of the Buddha, who lived thousands of years ago.

Some people say prayers as a way of talking to God. They may thank God, ask for help, or tell God how they are feeling.

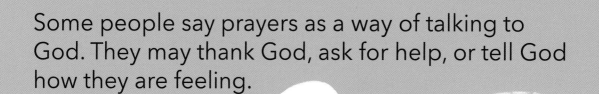

Some Muslims pray five times every day.

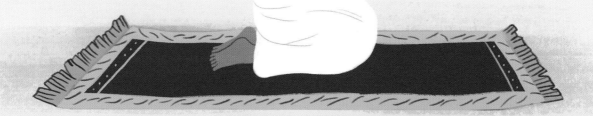

I am a Christian. I say my prayers every night, before I go to sleep.

People's beliefs can affect how and what they eat. Many Hindus do not eat meat because they believe all life is holy.

For Hindus, the cow is a special animal because it gives milk.

A gurdwara is a Sikh place of worship.
A vegetarian meal, called langar, is served
after worship for everyone to share.

We believe that
sharing food shows
that everyone is
equal in God's eyes.

Jewish people avoid eating some foods, such as pork, as
part of their religion.

We don't
eat shellfish,
either.

Some people wear special clothing to show their religion. Jewish men and boys wear a small cap called a kippah as a constant reminder of God.

I wear a prayer shawl when I pray.

Sikhs have five signs of their faith, called the Five Ks. One is kesh (uncut hair).

Many religions have special
books that are **holy** to them.

We are learning to
read the Qur'an.

Muslims believe the Qur'an is the word of Allah.
They treat this holy book with great respect.

The Christian holy book is the Bible. Part of it tells the story of Jesus's life.

At Christmas, we listen to the story of Jesus's birth.

My mom reads me a story about Rama and Sita at bedtime.

Hindus have many different holy books. The Ramayana tells stories about the god, Rama, and his wife, Sita.

Religions have special places where people go to meet and **worship**.

We have a service with hymns, prayers, and Bible readings.

Christians worship in a church.

Muslims worship at a mosque.

We hear the call to prayer from a tall tower called a minaret.

This is the Ark where the Torah scrolls are kept. The Torah is our holy book.

Jews worship at a synagogue.

19

Many Hindus worship at a mandir, or temple. They believe it is God's home on Earth.

We take our shoes off when we go in to show respect.

Inside a Sikh gurdwara is a copy of the Guru Granth Sahib.

The Guru Granth Sahib is our holy book.

We keep the Guru Granth Sahib covered when we are not reading it.

In a vihara, Buddhists make **offerings** to the Buddha.

We bow and offer flowers, candles, **and** incense.

Many people also worship at home. In most Hindu homes, there is a statue or picture of one or more of the gods.

We worship in our prayer room every day.

Shabbat is a day of rest and prayer for Jews. It begins on Friday night with a special family meal.

Festivals are times when people come together to celebrate. Many festivals remember special events in a religion's history.

At Christmas, Christians celebrate the birth of Jesus.

I love setting up the nativity **scene.**

They have special services in church, sing carols, give presents, and eat delicious food.

Eid-ul-Fitr is a special time for Muslims. It marks the end of Ramadan. This is a month when Muslims **fast** during the day.

At Eid, we wish each other "Eid Mubarak," which means "Happy Eid."

There are all kinds of special
times in people's everyday lives.

When a baby is born, a Muslim father whispers a prayer
in his baby's ear. Something sweet, such as date juice, is
put on the baby's tongue for a sweet and happy life.

In some Buddhist countries, boys become monks for a few months. Monks live simple lives and do acts of charity. In a ceremony, the boys' heads are shaved and they wear robes.

At a Sikh wedding, a hymn is sung as the couple walk around the Guru Granth Sahib.

People who do not follow a religion often share some of the same beliefs as religious people.

They believe in being kind, helping others, and treating people as they would like to be treated.

Everyone believes in something.
So, what do you believe?

Notes for teachers, parents, and caregivers

Buddhism

Buddhists follow the teachings of a man called Siddhartha Gautama, who became the Buddha, or "enlightened one." He lived around 2,500 years ago. Buddhists use his teachings as a guide for their lives, and as a way of understanding the realities of life. Buddhism is unique because, unlike many other religions, it is not based on a belief in a personal God who created and looks after the world. The Buddha did not claim to be a god and did not want to be worshiped as one.

Christianity

Christians believe in one God, and follow the teachings of Jesus, whom they call Christ. They believe that Jesus is the Son of God, sent to Earth to save people from their sins. During his life, Jesus taught people about God's love for them. Christians believe that Jesus was crucified, but that he rose from the dead and ascended into Heaven to be with God. This is called the Resurrection, and shows that death is not the end, but the start of a new life with God.

Hinduism

Hinduism is one of the oldest religions, with its roots in India more than 4,000 years ago. Today, there are around a billion Hindus. There are various ways of being a Hindu. Many Hindus believe in a great spirit, called Brahman. They sometimes call this spirit God. Hindus also worship gods and goddesses, who represent different aspects of Brahman's power. Hindus believe that every living thing has a soul (atman) which is reincarnated in another body when they die. This happens again and again until, by living a good life, you reach moksha, or freedom.

Islam

Islam is a religion whose followers are called Muslims. The word Islam means obedience, or submission, in Arabic. Muslims submit to the will of God, whom they call Allah, and follow Allah's guidance in their lives. Muslims believe that Allah sent messengers, called prophets, to teach people about Islam. The last and greatest of these was Muhammad who lived in Saudi Arabia around 1,400 years ago. Allah revealed the Qur'an, the holy book of Islam, to Muhammad.

Judaism

Judaism is the religion of the Jewish people. It is one of the world's oldest religions, dating back around 4,000 years. Jews believe in one God who created the world. According to the Torah (the Jewish holy book), God chose a man called Abraham to be the father of the Jews. They believe that God made a covenant (agreement) with Abraham. God promised to guide and care for the Jews, if they kept the laws that God had given to them and lived just and wise lives, loving God.

Sikhism

The Sikh religion began about 500 years ago in Punjab, India. At that time, the main religions of the region were Hinduism and Islam, but there were deep divisions between the two. Nanak, a holy man, introduced a new religion which promoted tolerance and equality. He became the first of ten Sikh gurus, or holy teachers. Sikhs believe in one God, and hope to grow closer to God through prayer and praise. Working hard, earning an honest living, and looking after other people are also important aspects of being a Sikh.

Websites for Parents and Educators

https://ed.ted.com/lessons/the-five-major-world-religions-john-bellaimey#watch
This TedEd video explores the history of the five major world religions and summarizes their beliefs and practices.

https://uri.org/kids/world-religions
An introduction to several of the world's religions and belief systems

Useful words

elders Older people who are important leaders and teachers of a religion

equal The same as

fast To go without food as part of worship in a religion

holy Linked to God and special to a religion

incense Sticks or cones that give off a sweet smell when burned

nativity To be born; representing the birth of Jesus

offerings Flowers, food, money, and other objects offered to God or a god

respect A feeling of great admiration for a person

worship Show devotion, for example, by saying prayers and singing songs

Index